Original title:
Life: A Series of Unfortunate Events

Copyright © 2025 Creative Arts Management OÜ
All rights reserved.

Author: Gabriel Kingsley
ISBN HARDBACK: 978-1-80566-009-5
ISBN PAPERBACK: 978-1-80566-304-1

Charcoal Skies and Moonlit Grief

In the chaos of the day, we laugh,
Chasing rainbows made of gaffes.
With every stumble, joy is spun,
Atop our heads, a silly bun.

Clouds might tumble, storms will brew,
But we'll dance like we always do.
With charcoal skies that paint our plight,
We'll giggle through the moony night.

A Canvas of Challenges

Life's a canvas, oh what fun,
Splattered colors, wild and run.
Each mistake, a brushstroke bold,
Stories of laughter, yet untold.

With every fall, we paint anew,
Splatters of joy in every hue.
Glimmers of hope in messy art,
With wink and chuckle, we take part.

Strands of Serendipity

Weaving tales of twisted fate,
Finding humor in the late.
Every knot a chance to cheer,
Through tangled threads, we persevere.

A slip, a trip, a hearty laugh,
In mishaps, we find the path.
Strands of luck, not what it seems,
Yet we dance in wildest dreams.

The Rise from Ashen Roots

From ashes sprung, a quirky cheer,
In the wreckage, we find our beer.
What's a fall without some grace?
We trip and laugh in this mad race.

With roots in chaos, up we go,
Blooming brightly from all our woes.
In every stumble, joy resides,
Through ash and blaze, the heart abides.

Fate's Unraveled Threads

Tangled yarn in a basket lay,
A cat pounced in, oh what a fray!
Knots of chaos, colors collide,
We laugh as our plans take a ride.

Socks go missing, where did they stray?
A sock goblin's feast, what can we say?
Barefoot shuffles on chilly floors,
We chuckle despite the open doors.

The Chronicles of Missteps

I tripped on a shoelace, fell in a heap,
The neighbor's dog giggled, oh what a beep!
Coffee spilled, a splash most divine,
A portrait of chaos, but still I shine!

Maps in hand, we wander astray,
Missed the left turn, now we ballet!
Bumps in the road, we dance along,
In our blunders, we all feel strong.

Whispers of a Broken Compass

My compass spins, like a dizzying dream,
North is now south; I start to scream!
The sun is my guide, or maybe the moon,
With each silly twist, I'll be home soon.

Directions from friends, all states are wrong,
But laughing provides the best travel song.
So here I am, lost and carefree,
Even in madness, I'm still so free!

The Dance of 1000 Follies

Join the dance, oh what a sight!
With two left feet, I twirl with delight.
Bumping the wall, I spin and sway,
Laughter erupts, come join the play!

Each misstep is but a joyful cheer,
A jiggle, a giggle, let's persevere!
The music gets louder, can't catch my breath,
In leaps and bounds, we dance with death!

When Laughter Masks the Tears

A banana peel upon the floor,
I trip and fall, hear laughter roar.
The world's a stage, I'm just a clown,
With every slip, I tumble down.

Coffee spills upon my shirt,
Yet still I smile, despite the hurt.
With every mishap, I find delight,
In clumsiness, my heart takes flight.

Unwritten Stories of Woe

Lost my keys, can't find my shoes,
I'd rather jump into some blues.
Each wrong turn, a laugh or two,
Like choosing ham when craving stew.

A bird once pooped right on my head,
I laughed it off and went to bed.
Each silly tale, a treasure trove,
In misadventure, we learn to rove.

The Poetry of Unwanted Surprises

Opened a gift, just socks inside,
But I wear them with foolish pride.
Each bizarre twist, a laugh on cue,
  At least it's better than a shoe!

A sneeze in public, oh what a sound,
A symphony where giggles abound.
Life's unexpected with jokes galore,
  We navigate this quirky chore.

Echoes of Hope in Dark Corners

In shadows lurk the silly beasts,
They dance and twirl, to say the least.
With every fumble, a heart that beams,
Even through chaos, we find dreams.

A paper cut, a comical plight,
Makes me chuckle, such a sight!
Amid the woes, we tend to cope,
Finding laughter, there's always hope.

A Symphony of Sighs

In a world where gadgets break,
Wires tangle, cakes just flake,
Each morning starts with a loud yawn,
And socks are lost as if they're gone.

A dog runs off with my shoes,
While birds play tricks, spreading the blues,
The coffee spills, a drip, a splash,
Yet here I sit, and laugh, then dash.

Through muddy puddles, I will leap,
While stubborn grass, it makes me weep,
Oh, joy, the serene sound of rain,
It pours, it floods, like sweet disdain.

But at the end of each long day,
I find small joys in disarray,
For every sigh, a giggle follows,
In this dance, life's sweetly swallows.

The Weight of Worn Wings

I tried to fly with paper wings,
But gravity has other things,
A gust of wind, my heart delight,
Ends up in awkward, clumsy flight.

The road is long, the shoes so tight,
I trip and stumble, a funny sight,
Yet through the falls and all the fumbles,
I rise again, through laughs and grumbles.

A bucket list of things to try,
Like cheese that squeaks and pickles that fly,
In every blunder, a lesson found,
That laughter's gold, and love's around.

So here I stand with wings so frayed,
In this grand mess, I won't be swayed,
For every weight my heart must bear,
A chuckle dances in the air.

Where the Wild Winds Blow

The winds whip wild, my hair a mess,
Chasing chaos, I must confess,
Umbrellas turn, like creatures strange,
And all around, the skies arranges.

Leaves swirl around, a joyful race,
As squirrels laugh, they set the pace,
Each gust a push to run and twirl,
Embracing fun in nature's whirl.

I seek the paths where laughter flows,
Where friends unite and joy just grows,
Through bumps and bruises, we will sing,
As life's oddities make hearts spring.

So let the wild winds blow today,
For in their dance, I find my way,
With every gust, I leap, I cheer,
For in this madness, love is near.

Fractured Dreams and Rusted Cages

In rusted cages dreams take flight,
But clumsy hands can't hold them tight,
I laugh at plans that fall apart,
As hiccups dance within my heart.

A broken clock that's stuck in time,
Rings out its bells, yet misses prime,
With every tick, a chance to fall,
Yet up I go, I heed its call.

Oh fractured dreams, let's play a game,
Where nothing stays quite as the same,
I'll chase the stars with goofy grace,
While giggles light this wacky space.

So if you see my dreams take wing,
Remember, none of this is king,
For through the cracks, a joy reveals,
That life is funny, and love heals.

Silver Linings in Gloom

When rain clouds gather, hearts can sink,
But puddles are just a chance to blink.
We slip and slide, and laugh out loud,
For clumsiness turns us into a crowd.

A tumble here, a stutter there,
Life's little mishaps become a fair.
With every fall, we raise a grin,
Finding joy in the mess we're in.

A Tapestry of Tumbles

Juggling tasks while tripping and swaying,
Even fails can be fun in the fraying.
We weave our blunders into bright threads,
Crafting a quilt from missteps and dreads.

With each new spill, we learn and grow,
Dancing through chaos, putting on a show.
Life's little oopsies spark our delight,
Turning fumbles into flights of light.

Through Storms and Shadows

Umbrellas are snapped, we dodge and weave,
Yet laughter remains, it's hard to believe.
In windy gusts, we find our pace,
Chasing rainbows with each clumsy chase.

The shadows loom, yet we boldly prance,
Dancing in puddles, giving fate a chance.
With every blunder, we strike a pose,
For in the gloom, the humor flows.

Embracing the Beautiful Chaos

When life throws pies that splatter and fly,
We wear the mess like a badge, oh my!
Embracing chaos, it's all in the fun,
Each stumble a memory, each mistake a pun.

Our hearts keep dancing, as spills take flight,
In laughter's embrace, everything feels right.
We twirl through madness, a merry old crew,
Finding beauty in chaos, in all that we do.

Threads of Gold

Once I ran to save my hat,
Tripped on a cat, how about that?
Gold threads twinkled in the sun,
Oh what a choice, here comes the fun!

Fell into a cake, face first,
Laughed so hard, I thought I'd burst.
Every slice a different fate,
Is this a meal, or just my state?

Chased a dream, fell into a tree,
Squirrel laughed, said, 'Let it be!'
Threads of gold or tangled mess,
Life's a stitch, I must confess.

But then I found a little prize,
A secret smile, a sly surprise.
So here's to joy in silly scorn,
With threads of gold, the heart is worn.

Worn with Time

The clock struck twelve, I missed my ride,
Stood like a statue, filled with pride.
Worn-out shoes and mismatched socks,
Tripping over puddles, dodging rocks.

Yesterday's toast still stuck on the floor,
Honey's a trap, I'll say no more.
Each twist and turn makes me laugh,
In this silly, worn-out path.

With wrinkles deep, and wobbly chairs,
Life throws gum and rusty snares.
Yet I dance in worn-out shoes,
Finding fun in silly blues.

So wear that smile, though time may scold,
There's laughter found in threads of old.
With every mishap, ugly or fine,
We paint our hearts, forever worn with time.

Echoes of What Could Have Been

I once thought I'd be a star,
Instead, I'm here, just drinking tar.
Echoes whisper in the night,
What if that dress was just too tight?

Planned a feast, ended with stew,
Burnt my toast, what could I do?
Echoes laugh from every dish,
What could have been, just a foolish wish.

Frolicked with dreams, they slipped away,
How do I make this old cat stay?
Promises dance like shadows bold,
In echoes soft of stories told.

So here I am, with quirks so keen,
Saluting the ghosts of things unseen.
Raise a glass to the surreal and then,
Toast to laughs—for that could have been!

The Haunting of Missed Chances

At midnight came a ghostly sigh,
Missed my chance, oh my, oh my!
Wandered paths I did not tread,
Spilled my tea, not a word said.

A game of darts became my plight,
Stuck the board, oh what a sight!
Booing echoes from my friends,
This haunting never really ends.

Thought I'd call, but lost my phone,
Instead, I sung to a garden gnome.
With missed chances creeping near,
I laughed in the face of silly fear.

So here's to ghosts, both faint and fair,
They remind me of the fun we share.
In every misstep, let's make a dance,
For in this haunt lies the happiest chance!

Whispers of Woe

Beneath the quiet of a sigh,
Whispers dance, passing by.
Found my keys inside the fridge,
Thought I'd cook, but what a bridge!

Muffins burned, but spirits rose,
With every flop, the laughter grows.
Whispers flirt with every fall,
Each little mishap tells it all.

A paper cut from dreams I penned,
Whispers tease, 'You should pretend!'
So here's to woes that twist and twirl,
In this merry, quirky swirl.

With every stumble, take a bow,
For whispers of woe teach me how.
A giggle tucked in every wry,
In falls and flops, we learn to fly.

Uninvited Guests of Tomorrow

They crash the party with no invite,
Eating your snacks, what a sight!
Bringing their chaos, a jolly mess,
Each moment with them feels like stress.

Yet laughter lingers, a silly dance,
With jokes and blunders, they take a chance.
Every mishap, a tale to spin,
Uninvited can still let fun in.

So raise a toast to things that stray,
To guests who come, come what may.
In the end, it's the fun we keep,
Turns out, these guests don't let us sleep.

From spills to thrills, let's have a ball,
With uninvited friends, we have a call.
Tomorrow's clouds may rain or shine,
With these guests, we always dine fine.

Portraits of Perseverance

In every stumble, a story grows,
Brushing off dirt, we strike a pose.
With paint of laughter, we color our fate,
Each canvas splattered with joy and weight.

Though brushes slip and colors run,
We giggle at mishaps, thank the sun.
Each portrait shows a heart that's bold,
In the gallery of life, watch it unfold.

With every line drawn, we stand proud,
A motley crew, we cheer aloud.
In the art of living, imperfections gleam,
Portraits of struggle are part of the dream.

So hang them high, these quirky sights,
Celebrate courage with all our might.
In the gallery of ups and downs,
We wear our misfortunes like crowns.

The Veil of Fateful Turns

Behind every door, a twist awaits,
A riddle wrapped in fate's strange traits.
With uncertainty, we play our game,
Each turn leads to laughter, none the same.

From kitchen fires to accidental falls,
We navigate through life's wily halls.
Trading sorrows for chuckles bright,
In moments of mishap, we feel the light.

Fateful turns may lead us wrong,
But find the humor, and we'll belong.
With every plot twist, a giggle grows,
In life's comedy, see how it flows.

So raise a glass to paths unsure,
To unexpected swaps that feel so pure.
Behind every veil, let laughter churn,
In this tangled dance, for joy we yearn.

Splintered Paths and Twisted Roads

With every fork, we choose our way,
Through splintered paths where sprites play.
Each bumpy ride, a truckload of glee,
Driving down a path not meant to be.

Tangled branches block our sight,
Yet we forge ahead, our spirits bright.
With every wrong turn, a story to tell,
Of adventures forged amidst the swell.

Twisted roads may lead to fiascos,
But fear not the laughter, it surely grows.
Every detour a dance, every stop a song,
In this wacky journey, we all belong.

So let's embrace the strange and wild,
Like a carefree parent with a quirky child.
For in these splinters, the fun unfolds,
Life's merry chaos, in laughter, it holds.

Wintry Winds and Unraveled Threads

In winter's grip, we trip and slide,
A tangle here, a misplaced stride.
With every gust, we find a way,
To laugh instead of rue the day.

A snowball thrown, it's all in fun,
But here comes trouble, oh what a run!
The thermals fail, the hats take flight,
We stumble back with pure delight.

Our scarves entwined like lovers lost,
A game of tug, not quite the cost.
In frosty air, our giggles bloom,
As visions of warmth begin to loom.

Each slip and slide, a tale to tell,
A wintry song of joy to swell.
For every fall, a chuckle bled,
Unraveled threads, yet hope is fed.

Portrait of a Hopeful Heart

A canvas bright with colors bold,
Yet splashes land, oh how uncontrolled!
With every brush, our dreams collide,
A funny mess, but joy won't hide.

The sun may set, the shadows creep,
But in each heart, a giggle seeps.
Mistakes are just the art of play,
A hopeful tune to lead the way.

A crooked smile, a dopey grin,
The portrait sings where flaws begin.
Brush strokes wild, the laughter swells,
In every bump, a story dwells.

So hang it high, this happy plight,
With every beat, our souls ignite.
For hope's a dance, a joyful dart,
In colorful lines, the hopeful heart.

Reflections of Resilience

In puddles deep, reflections show,
Of misfits born from joy and woe.
A splash, a laugh, we see anew,
Our hearts, like rainbows, break on through.

We bounce and tip, we flip and glide,
Through every slip, we laugh with pride.
Life's rippled mirror, a comic face,
With every stumble, we find our place.

Like rubber ducks, we bobbing float,
Through storms and mess with a little gloat.
Resilient souls with glimmers bright,
In every wrong, we find the light.

So let it rain, let torrents pour,
We'll dance through puddles evermore.
With every drop, we'll share the fun,
In reflections bold, we all are one.

Chasing Shadows of Yesterday

In corners dim, where echoes play,
We chase the shadows of yesterday.
Each footfall sounds like laughter's tune,
A quirky dance beneath the moon.

With every step, a memory slips,
A clumsy glide, like wayward ships.
In playful spins, we lose our way,
Yet find the joy in the dismay.

We seek the past in chuckles bright,
For yesterday's tales bring pure delight.
A wink, a nod, a silly prank,
In shadows deep, our hearts still clank.

So onward we run, with love in tow,
Chasing old whispers, our spirits glow.
For in each laugh, the future blends,
And shadows fade, but joy transcends.

Ashes of Unfulfilled Promises

In a world where plans go astray,
Expectations trip in a funny ballet.
Dreams like balloons that drift and deflate,
We chuckle as fate plays a bizarre weight.

The puppy-chewed list of things we would do,
Turns into a pile of papers askew.
With each flopped idea, we can't help but laugh,
At the folly of paths mapped out on our path.

Mocking hopes dashed in a comedic dance,
Life throws pies, but we still take a chance.
For every mishap, a grin starts to spread,
In the foolishness, joy finds its thread.

So raise a glass to the plans we forgot,
In the life of the not-so-serious plot.
With smiles and laughter, our hearts carry weight,
In the ashes of promises, we'll still celebrate!

The Flicker of Resilient Sparks

When troubles arise like mischievous sprites,
We dance through the chaos, embracing the sights.
Each stumble a jig, each slip a surprise,
We twirl through the mess, with stars in our eyes.

With every setback, our spirits ignite,
In the forge of mishaps, we shine ever bright.
For a giggle's a spark in a thunderous storm,
We'll coax out the laughs, let the norm be reborn.

Life sends us spirals like playful wild darts,
Yet here we stand, with resilient hearts.
We'll gather our humor and chase off the gloom,
In the flicker of sparks, let the joy find its room.

So when the world trips, and the rubber bands snap,
We share all our stories, a funny mishap.
In the glow of our laughter, we rise from the dark,
Let's dance in the chaos, let's make our own mark!

When Stars Align in Shadows

In a twist where the good meets the quirky absurd,
The universe chuckles, not saying a word.
As stars take a tumble, they giggle and fall,
And out of the shadows, we stumble and crawl.

The universe winks with a sly, playful grin,
As we trip over fate like a puppy with spin.
A mishap is magic, with laughter as glue,
In the chaos of chance, we blossom anew.

So when the night holds its cloak tight and deep,
We'll gather our dreams, let the shadows all leap.
Though our plans may get twisted like spaghetti on plates,
We laugh as we feast on the quirks that fate states.

With a toast to the stars that may lead us astray,
We'll rejoice in the journey, come what may.
For in the darkness, a light starts to glow,
When shadows align, let the laughter bestow!

The Tears that Water the Garden

With tears like rain in a comedic drizzle,
We tend to our garden, where humor can sizzle.
Each drop tells a tale of a moment gone wrong,
Yet blooms of good laughter grow steady and strong.

The weeping willow shares wisdom and glee,
A giggle escapes as we prune the root tree.
In the puddles of sorrow, we find the best cheer,
With each silly slip, we plant dreams that endear.

From the weeds of mishaps, bright flowers emerge,
As we dance in the mud, with laughter we surge.
In the chaos of growth, in each slip of our heart,
We cultivate joy, our masterpiece art.

So here's to the tears that sow seeds in delight,
In the garden of folly, we ever take flight.
With humor as sunshine, our roots will take hold,
In the tears that water, our stories unfold!

Serendipity Amongst the Misfires

Tripped on a shoelace, fell with a grunt,
Coffee spilled loudly, oh what a stunt!
Yet a friend laughed loud, shared a great snack,
In our silly chaos, there's nothing we lack.

Lost my keys again, must be a trend,
Husband finds them, 'How do you spend?
Life's little messes bring giggles and sighs,
In this wild ride, we find the surprise!

Umbrellas flipped inside-out, what a sight!
Dance in the rain, oh what pure delight!
Each little mishap, a gift wrapped in cheer,
Finding joy in the odd, as we persevere.

With laughter we gather, tales that we weave,
In a world full of stumbles, we choose to believe.
Misfires are funny, we hold our heads high,
Serendipity shines, like stars in the sky.

Resilience in the Face of Adversity

Fell off my bike, scraped knee on the grass,
Instead of tears, I just laugh at the class!
The crowd gathered round, offered me ice,
With giggles in tow, life's simple device.

Burnt toast for breakfast, oh, what a feat,
Crispy little black squares, a morning treat!
Yet stir-fried surprises await us in store,
With charred little crunch, who could ask for more?

Rain poured on my plans, what can you do?
Danced inside puddles, just me and my shoes!
Each droplet a tune in this whimsical play,
Resilience is funny, come join in the sway.

Things fall apart, that's a natural way,
But we laugh a little harder, day after day.
With each little mishap, we find room to grow,
Resilience is sparkly, as we put on a show.

An Odyssey of Misfortune

Packed up my bag, left the house behind,
Right then a bird, my sandwich it fined!
Chased off that critter, I laughed at the test,
With crumbs on my shirt, I still feel blessed.

Lost in the traffic, my GPS spun,
Pulsing like disco, oh what silly fun!
Wound up at a diner, the fries were just grand,
Sometimes misfortune leads to snacks, just as planned.

Weather turned wild, skies dressed up in grey,
Met up with a friend, let's make it a play!
We built little forts with the chairs in a row,
An odyssey's laughter is how we both glow.

Maps can lead astray, while journeys can mix,
But we stitch tales together, with laughter that sticks.
In fortune or mischief, we'll wade through the strife,
An odyssey laughs at the chaos of life.

Painted with Shades of Misery

Stumbled on stairs, walked right into a wall,
Painted with shades where my ego took a fall.
But oh, with the bruises, I learned a new way,
To humor the clumsy, and dance in the fray.

A bright sunny morning turned rainy and wet,
As I slipped on my socks, and land on the pet!
Yet giggles erupted, my spirits took flight,
In shadows of misery, the laughter feels right.

Grapes turned to raisins, left out in the sun,
Like plans that unravel, just trying to run.
With life's little failures, each one a delight,
Painted with laughter, we color the night.

Adventures in chaos, asking for more,
We bask in the silly, the fun we adore.
With paintbrushes soggy, and shades that mislead,
In the crosshairs of trouble, it's joy that we need.

A Dance with Misfortune

I tripped on my shoelace, oh what a sight,
The crowd erupted, laughter took flight.
A twist, a spin, I hope to impress,
But ended up sprawled in my Sunday best.

With banana peels lurking on every street,
I waltz through mishaps, a two-left-feet treat.
A tumble here, a slip there, all while I prance,
Misfortune and I are locked in a dance.

I spilled my drink right onto my date,
But she laughed it off, as if it were fate.
We laughed 'til we cried at the chaos around,
In the ballroom of blunders, joy can be found.

So here's to the flops, the stumbles, the falls,
In the grand scheme of life, let's embrace the brawls.
With a twirl and a chuckle, we'll take to the stage,
For dancing with misfortune is all the rage!

The Art of Falling Down

They say grace is key in the dance of life's game,
But watch me trip into the hall of fame.
A misstep, a plunge, down I go with flair,
With a flip and a roll, I land without a care.

I practiced my balance on a tightrope of fate,
But gravity laughed, and I couldn't wait.
Over popcorn and drinks, I soared through the air,
A masterpiece framed by a crowd in despair.

But what's a good fall without some good cheer?
The audience roared, their laughter sincere.
With each awkward tumble, I'm crafting a skill,
For the art of falling down gives me quite the thrill.

So let's raise a toast to the chaos abound,
To the many fine ways we can fall to the ground.
With a wink and a smile, I'll take the next chance,
For stumbling through life can still make you dance!

Every Silver Has Its Cloud

In the glimmer of silver, a cloud knocked me down,
I stepped in a puddle, now I'm queen of the town.
With a soggy shoe squelch and a chuckle of glee,
Life's little blunders are a comedy spree.

I found a lost penny; up went my hopes,
Until I discovered it's stuck in the ropes.
A treasure foretold turned to tangled despair,
Guess I'll need scissors or a whole lot of prayer.

While sunshine and laughter seem seldom to meet,
The rainbow arises from my muddy defeat.
For every small failure, there's giggling around,
Beneath heavy clouds, a new joy can be found.

So collect all your mishaps, wear your fumbles proud,
In the dance of existence, every silver has cloud.
With humor as armor, we'll weather the storm,
For a life filled with laughter is infinitely warm!

When Rain Falls on Parades

Oh glorious day, our parade's on display,
But then came the downpour, it washes away.
Umbrellas go flying, and floats start to sink,
While dancers slip-slide in a puddle of ink.

The band plays along despite drizzle and dread,
Marching through raindrops, they forge ahead.
With laughter and splashes, we move through the muck
When rain falls on parades, we'll just laugh at our luck

So let's crank up the fun, let's twirl in the storm,
For a wet celebration can still feel like warm.
With joy in our hearts, we won't be dismayed,
When life sends us rain, we'll make lemonade.

Raise your soggy banner, shake off that despair,
For the fun comes alive when the sky isn't fair.
With a skip and a grin, we'll dance in the rain,
When parades meet a downpour, there's always a gain!

Shadows that Cling to Dreams

In the corner, shadows creep,
Whispering secrets we can't keep.
They giggle as we chase the light,
Fools believing dreams take flight.

Chasing figures in the night,
They dance away, what a sight!
With a hop, skip, and a fall,
Who said dreams are worth it all?

Cupcakes flipped and frogs that sing,
Life's a carnival, not a ring.
Hold tight to laughter, let it gleam,
Shadows haunt just to redeem.

As we stumble, trip, and slide,
The shadows laugh, we cannot hide.
In this merry game of fate,
We'll take a bow and celebrate!

When Fortune Winks and Blinks

Fortune winks with a cheeky grin,
Then turns her back as we begin.
With every step, we trip and fall,
Just her way of having a ball.

A scratch on luck, a dent on chance,
Fortune leads in a comical dance.
With a wink here, a blink there,
We're tangled in her playful snare.

Like squirrels in a game of chase,
We dash around, but lose the race.
Yet laughter echoes through our plight,
As we tumble, it feels just right.

So raise a glass to twisted fate,
With each mishap, we celebrate!
When fortune plays, we join the show,
In a funny tale of high and low.

The Paradox of Hopeful Despair

In a garden of hopeful tears,
We sow the seeds of our big fears.
With every bloom, a twisted smile,
Despair and hope dance for a while.

We wear our hearts with a silly frown,
As life spins us round and round.
Holding hands with doubt's embrace,
Yet joy sneaks in to join the race.

With shoes untied and plans gone wild,
We skip along like a carefree child.
In paradox, we find our cheer,
In hopeful despair, we persevere.

So here's to laughter, here's to tears,
In the greatest mess, we find our peers.
For every laugh that hides a groan,
We'll toast to chaos, it's all our own!

Navigating the Desert of Lost Dreams

In the desert of dreams gone dry,
We search for mirages as they fly.
Sipping air in the sun's cruel gaze,
Lost among the never-ending haze.

We build castles from shifting sand,
Only to watch them slip from hand.
Yet each tumble brings a grin,
As we trip and laugh, letting joy in.

With cacti waving like old friends,
They poke at hope that never ends.
Through the swirls of dust and sun,
We find that laughter is the real fun.

So here's our map marked with delight,
As we wander through day and night.
In the desert, with every beam,
We find a way to chase our dream!

Unraveling Thread of Fate

In a world of tangled strings,
We weave our awkward webs,
Each knot tells tales of clumsiness,
Like shoestrings, tripping two-step ebbs.

With spoons that bend and forks that twist,
We dine on life's odd feast,
Spilled mustard on our Sunday best,
Uninvited chaos, yet we're pleased.

Through hiccups, stumbles, fumbles too,
We laugh and take a bow,
For every time we fall anew,
A dance of folly, take a vow.

So here's to fate and its grand jest,
The mishaps that bring joy,
In the funny chaos, we find our rest,
A punchline in the ploy.

The Beauty in Brokenness

Cracked mugs and missing socks,
Our treasures lie askew,
We embrace the mismatched clocks,
Time tickles us, it's true.

Jigsaw puzzles without a piece,
The cats nap on the floor,
We find our screw-ups bring us ease,
A symphony we can't ignore.

Laughter bubbles from within,
As we juggle crazy roles,
In every loss, a chance to win,
A heart that joyfully consoles.

With flaws that dance upon our skin,
We're perfectly imperfectly made,
A joyful mess beneath our grin,
In brokenness, hope's not delayed.

Chasing Storms and Sunsets

With umbrellas tossed and hats askew,
We run from clouds that scold,
Yet rainbows peak through, just for a view,
A silver lining brightly told.

Sunsets blaze while storms do chase,
We twirl in puddles, splash and spill,
In nature's dance, we find our place,
Each drop a laugh, a joyous thrill.

Lightning flashes the night's soft grin,
We banter with the howling gales,
With every storm, a fresh begin,
Dancing till the daylight pales.

So here's to skies both dark and bright,
To every twist and turn we take,
Through stormy nights, we find our light,
A merry heart, for laughter's sake.

Echoes of Bleak Beginnings

From stumbles that begin our tales,
To moments filled with crudely glee,
Our footsteps leave behind some trails,
In mishaps, we find our decree.

With mismatched socks and coffee stains,
We crown ourselves the clumsy kings,
In every fumble, joy remains,
Life's silly dance, oh what it brings!

A fruitcake gifted, shape of a shoe,
We nibble and we laugh so loud,
For awkwardness is something we do,
Clumsy moments, we're so proud.

So raise a glass to wobbly starts,
To mischief wrapped in warm embrace,
Within this chaos, love imparts,
Echoes of joy, a silly grace.

Journey Through Tempestuous Hearts

In the dance of daily mishaps,
Where laughter often collides,
We trip and juggle our laughter,
As fortune takes us on wild rides.

Coffee spills on my new shirt,
A cat on my head leads the way,
With every stutter and squawk,
I find joy in disarray.

Tripping over my own two feet,
The universe plays its tricks,
We stumble and roll on the floor,
Dodging one misfortune after six.

Yet through the chaos and the mess,
We find our hearts full and light,
For in each bump and each blunder,
There's a spark of pure delight.

Fractals of Frustration

Like fractals drawn with shaky hands,
Life twists in curious ways,
A GPS that's lost its map,
Leading us in a daze.

Forgotten keys and broken phones,
I laugh while cleaning my mess,
Oh, the trials that turn to tales,
In life's comedic jest.

We try to walk a straightened path,
But life veers with silly bends,
We muse on how we seem to glide,
Through a maze where chaos blends.

Yet every fumble brings a smile,
Each blunder, a lively cheer,
For in the webs we often weave,
Fractals shimmer bright and near.

Paintings of a Shattered Mirror

Glimpses through the fractured glass,
Reveal the humor in our plight,
Each shard reflects a goofy grin,
As mirrors shimmer with delight.

Cracked reflections tell no lies,
A double vision, often absurd,
Missing socks and burnt toast for breakfast,
The gallery of marvelous blurred.

Every paint stroke, a mishap bright,
In the masterpiece of the day,
Misfortunes add an artist's touch,
To the canvas, come what may.

So we gather our cracks and flaws,
And hang them in the light anew,
For every laugh that breaks our fall,
Adds color to our view.

The Intricacies of Unluck

In a world where rain falls up,
And coffee brews wrong every time,
We navigate the oddities,
Finding humor in every rhyme.

Buttons pop, and shoes untie,
A wild chase down the street,
Yet each twist of fate we laugh,
At every funny defeat.

Life's a game of sorry cards,
And one-eyed dice tossed with glee,
In each clumsy maneuver we make,
A splash of joy — can't you see?

So let's cherish the hiccups dear,
And toast to woes that tickle our hearts,
For in the intricate dance of unluck,
Laughter's the sweetest of arts.

Threads of Fate in Tornado Skirts

In a whirlwind of chaos, I spin and twirl,
My plans take flight like a wayward girl.
A sock on the ceiling, a shoe in a tree,
Oh, what fun chaos brings to me!

Dinner's burnt offerings, the cat's on parade,
Lost my last cookie beneath the cascade.
With mismatched socks and hair in a mess,
Who knew a day could be such a jest?

The toast pops up playing a tune so sweet,
But I'm dancing with worry, tripping on my feet.
The universe chuckles, I join in the fray,
Embracing the quirks in this wild cabaret!

So here's to the storm, the laughter it brings,
To life's little hiccups and silly old things.
With tornado skirts flying, I'll answer the call,
For in every mishap, there's joy after all!

The Light That Fades at Dusk

As the sun dips low and the shadows creep,
Half-knitting a scarf, I find I can't sleep.
The kettle's on fire, the cat's in a pout,
Sometimes I wonder what it's all about.

The toast gets stuck, jamming up my cheer,
While fuzzy socks dance, I've lost my left ear.
Oh, the dimming light pretties all my flaws,
It's a circus of clumsiness, and I'm the applause!

Each moment's a puzzle, I struggle to find,
But giggles keep coming, it's surely divine.
With stars up above and dishes in stacks,
I'll toast to tomorrow and pounce on the snacks!

So here's to the dusk, to the funny little bends,
Where laughter awaits and the silliness blends.
In the fading light, I'll dance and I'll sway,
Finding joy in the night, and sweeping woes away!

A Chronicle of Cast-Off Wishes

On a comet of wishes, I throw out my dreams,
But they all come back with absurd little schemes.
A wish for a fortune brings only a flat,
And every grand scheme just leads to my cat.

Like socks in the dryer, they vanish in pairs,
My hopes flit away, like feathers in the air.
A pancake-shaped planet spins round in my mind,
While I trip on the stairs, just one of those blind.

With wishes gone wild, the cake's finally burnt,
As I forfeit my calls, my plans all invert.
Yet in every mishap, there's laughter to find,
A giggle erupts, oh the joy it unwinds!

So here's to the wishes that lead us astray,
To the topsy-turvy, come what may.
With a heart full of chuckles, I'll take on the plight,
For a world of whimsy is a treasure so bright!

Scribbles of Sorrowful Joy

With scribbles of joy, I doodle my plight,
Falling down stairs, oh, what a sight!
I chuckle through blunders, like paint on my nose,
Crafting my troubles into art no one knows.

In puddles of laughter, I splash and I grin,
My tangle of thoughts slips right under my skin.
A sprinkle of chaos, a dash of the wrong,
Turns each sour note into a comical song!

The toaster sings loudly and pops up its cheer,
While I dance like a fool, drowning out all my fear.
With each little mishap, I flow with the tide,
Collecting my giggles, my heart open wide.

So here's to the scribbles, the messy delights,
To the sorrowful joy that keeps us in fights.
For in every misstep, and every smirk bright,
Lives a flicker of fun, in the darkest of nights!

Navigating Life's Potholes

Bumping down the road so wide,
Hurdles up and down we glide.
With a grin and silly cheer,
We dodge the mess, hold laughter near.

Trip once, and trip again,
Find joy in every pain.
Roll in mud, but who cares,
We're slick with giggles and wild flares.

Through puddles splashing, we embrace,
A wobbly dance in the oddest place.
Over every bump, we leap and twirl,
Navigating life in a merry whirl.

So raise a toast to our grand ride,
With laughter and snacks stacked up inside.
For every misstep we claim with grace,
Is just a chapter in our funny chase.

The Symphony of Chaotic Moments

A trumpet blast and pots that clang,
Socks mismatched, the doorbell sang.
Chasing cats, oh what a sight,
Echoes of chaos, pure delight!

The clock is late, my pants are torn,
Yet through the storm, I was reborn.
Dance in circles, spin around,
In this madness, joy is found.

Each fumble strikes a chord so clear,
A silly laughter fills the ear.
With every laugh, a note we weave,
In this symphony, we believe!

So join the band of clumsy souls,
With air guitar and laughter's tolls.
We'll play our hearts through every scene,
As life's wild tune becomes our dream.

In the Wake of Disasters

Spilled the drink, oh what a mess!
Wipe it quick, in sheer distress.
A fallen cake, a broken shoe,
Yet here we stand, in laughter too.

From kitchen fires to wild bird flights,
We face it all without the fright.
With every mishap, we learn to cheer,
For disasters bring us closer here.

A missing sock, a pop of fate,
In every blunder, we celebrate.
So let the world spin out of track,
We'll wear our smiles, no turning back!

With each small fail, a story grows,
In every laugh, the friendship flows.
Let's paint the canvas, bright and bold,
In the wake of disaster, we find gold.

Stumbling Through Serendipity

A trip, a fall, then laughter loud,
While dancing beneath the clumsy cloud.
Falling into a pot of jam,
Sweetened by fate, there's no need to slam.

Each twirl in puddles, a joyful spree,
Like a wobbly bird, wild and free.
Glimpses of fortune in every mishap,
We wear our smiles like a joyful cap.

With every misstep, more fun we find,
Serendipity's wink is so very kind.
Through all the fumbles, we spin and sway,
In this odd dance, we'll find our way.

So here's to the stumbles that bring us glee,
In life's wild ride, we're meant to be!
With every laugh, we raise our glass,
To the beautiful chaos, may it ever last!

The Color of Faded Hopes

In a world where rainbows bend,
The light turned sour, not a friend.
Every dream can spill and fall,
Yet still we giggle through it all.

We paint with hues that fade away,
A canvas of mishaps on display.
Umbrellas turned inside out,
We twirl and spin, still causing doubt.

With every stumble, we arise,
Grinning bright, we fake our cries.
For what's a trip without some cheer,
A splash of joy in every tear?

So raise a glass to dreams gone wrong,
We'll dance to the tune of a silly song.
For hope may fade, its colors smudge,
But oh, we laugh, and we won't budge.

Tides of Trouble

The waves come crashing, oh so bold,
But laughter's warmth makes us feel gold.
We ride the tides, both up and down,
Wearing our smiles like a crown.

A surfboard's fickle, what a ride,
With every wave, we slip and glide.
But splashes make the best of friends,
In sea of woes, the laughter never ends.

Each tumble spins us into glee,
The ocean roars, but we are free.
For trouble's just a playful wave,
A chance to dance, a chance to rave.

So here's to storms and sandy shores,
With salty air to cure our sores.
With every tide, we shout and cheer,
For in this mess, we find our sphere.

Footprints in Soft Earth

With every step, we sink and sway,
In muddy patches, we find our way.
Our shoes may get stuck, but we don't care,
For laughter trails, light as air.

Squish and squash, we hear the sounds,
As luck's missteps dance around.
Each footprint echoes silly tales,
Of misadventures and wild gales.

The earth beneath may choose to cling,
But we just giggle and play the swing.
For every slip, there's joy and fun,
In every mess, we come undone.

So tiptoe through this muddy plot,
Embrace the muck, let troubles rot.
For in the dirt, we roam and cheer,
With footprints brightening the drear.

Beneath a Shattered Sky

We wander 'neath a roof of holes,
As raindrops plink on our poor soles.
With every drip, we laugh and sing,
A broken sky can still give bling.

Clouds may grumble, thunder rolls,
But we make jokes that soothe our souls.
For every crack lets sunshine in,
A silver lining fit for a grin.

With umbrellas turned inside out,
We dance in puddles, without a doubt.
For shattered skies won't dim our light,
We'll twirl and spin till day turns night.

So here's to skies that fall apart,
We'll mend them with our joyful heart.
For in the chaos, we will play,
And find the funny in dismay.

Brittle Dreams in Fractured Times

In a world where plans fall flat,
We dance with fate, a silly chat.
A kite that flies with no real string,
We laugh and cry at everything.

Coffee spills on a brand-new dress,
We grumble but it's really a mess.
Upside-down, we twirl and spin,
With a wink, we let the chaos in.

Plans unraveled, a jigsaw tease,
Stumbling through like autumn leaves.
Yet in the storm, we find our cheer,
Brittle dreams, we'll hold them near.

Through tangled paths, we make a scene,
In fractured times, we keep it clean.
With laughter loud and spirits bright,
We carry on through day and night.

The Art of Falling Gracefully

Stumbling in heels, oh what a sight,
A ballet dancer, sans the light.
Trip over air, a graceful dive,
With every tumble, we feel alive.

In a crowded room, we're the stars,
Our comic timing, just like guitars.
The floor is lava, we leap and bound,
In perfect chaos, joy is found.

With every slip, we learn and laugh,
A life of clumsiness, our true craft.
When ego bruises, the heart still sings,
In the art of falling, joy it brings.

So here's to wobbles, fumbles too,
The world is silly; embrace the skew.
In the dance of life, we can't depart,
For falling gently is quite the art.

Misadventures in Wonderment

Every corner hides a twisty fate,
Curiosity knocks, we can't be late.
Exploring paths we never planned,
In this mischief, we take a stand.

A treasure map that leads to snacks,
Unexpected joy amidst the cracks.
Chasing shadows, we grin and roam,
In misadventures, we find our home.

Lemonade spills on the summer grass,
A sticky mess but we laugh it up fast.
The world is weird; we're in the flow,
With every stumble, we let it show.

So let's embrace the odd and strange,
In this circus ride of happy change.
With wide-eyed glee, we'll dance and skip,
In misadventures, we find our grip.

Lessons from Life's Pratfalls

With every trip, a lesson learned,
From slip-ups made and bridges burned.
We giggle loudly, brush off the dirt,
In moments silly, we feel no hurt.

A rollercoaster ride of ups and downs,
We wear our smiles, not sad frowns.
Every pratfall, a tale to tell,
In humorous light, we cast our spell.

Falling forward, we find our way,
In a world that loves to play.
So here's to jests and goofy shocks,
In the greatest show, we're paradoxes.

With every misstep, we rise anew,
In twinkling laughter, we break on through.
Lessons taught in the silliest ways,
We honor the blunders of our days.

The Weight of Unseen Burdens

A bird on my shoulder, it's heavy, oh dear,
I tripped on my shoe lace, fell flat with a cheer.
Thought I could dance, but my feet had a plan,
Each twirl turned to stumble, then laughter began.

The groceries tumbled, my bag was a wreck,
I chased after cabbage, dodged right, then a peck.
With every misstep, I'd giggle and sigh,
Finding joy in the chaos, oh me, oh my!

My coffee just splashed, a most splendid mess,
It swirled like a fountain, I cannot confess.
The world keeps on turning, I take it in stride,
With invisible burdens, there's fun to abide.

So raise up your glass, to the slips and the tricks,
For laughter is golden, and humor can fix.
We'll waddle through stumbles, with friends by our side,
Through burdens unspoken, in smiles we abide.

Reflections in a Cracked Mirror

I stood in the bathroom, took a look at my face,
That mirror, it laughed, with a crack in its grace.
I grinned at the stranger, half-blinked, then I knew,
The ghost in the glass wore a better shade too.

My hair had more volume, like a squirrel in spring,
I tried to tame it, but it gave up on bling.
Each attempt through a brush just resulted in frizz,
And the mirror kept chuckling, how rude, how it is!

The reflection danced wildly, like it had no care,
Whispering secrets of how I should wear.
With toothpaste as lipstick, I took on the day,
A riot of color, in a humorous way.

So here's to the cracks that reflect all the fun,
For finding the beauty in chaos is won.
When life gives you mirrors, cracked comforts be near,
Embrace every giggle, and banish your fear!

Journeys Through Fields of Thorns

I wandered through roses, oh so sweet and bright,
But hidden behind blooms were thorns with a bite.
A step here, a scratch there, I giggled in pain,
"Next time wear armor!" I'd cry out in vain.

The bees buzzed around me, like they'd lost all their way,

I was the unsuspecting, a flower's buffet.
They danced with my curls, while I ducked and I swayed,

"Why do I dance here? My charm's been betrayed!"

But amidst every thorn, laughter sprang up,
Each prick was a joke, filling my half cup.
With petals a-flying and Mockingbird's tunes,
I tiptoed through trials beneath laughter-filled moons.

So here's to the thorns that make journeys so grand,
For bouncing through prickers, a challenge so bland.
With humor as armor, we forge on to roam,
Through fields ripe with folly, adventures call home.

The Light Between the Cracks

There's light in the shadows, a glimmer of hope,
In cracks of the sidewalk, we learn how to cope.
With every small fracture, a story unfolds,
Of giggles and shenanigans, shining like gold.

I stumbled on laughter, it sprouted like weeds,
A joke in the pavement, where humor proceeds.
In every misstep, with grace I had none,
Yet still, I was twirling, like I was the sun.

Through gaps in the pavement, I spied silly sights,
A cat doing yoga, oh what funny nights!
With every odd moment, a chuckle took flight,
Finding joy in the puzzling, heartily bright.

So cherish the cracks, where the light claims its space,
For humor keeps us in this quirky embrace.
With warmth through each laugh, we conquer the night,
In the light of the cracks, we find what feels right.

The Twilight of Forgotten Fables

In a town where the odd does bloom,
Cats wear hats, while dogs use a broom.
A chef who burns water, oh what a feat,
And squirrels hold meetings on how to cheat.

The clock declares noon at half-past three,
And umbrellas sprout wings as they flee.
Each sidewalk has stories, but none make sense,
Yet laughter erupts, and joy is immense.

A penguin slides by on a skateboard so slick,
While llamas compete in a dance-off chic.
With hiccups that echo through gardens of plight,
The world spins in humor, a comical sight.

So raise up a glass filled with lemonade,
To moments that sparkle, won't ever fade.
In the twilight we laugh, in the brightest of fables,
And grin at mishaps that life always labels.

Embracing the Uncanny Unknown

The sun wears a bowtie, oh what a joke,
While shadows conspire, and daisies poke.
A rabbit with spectacles reads the news,
In a world where the weird is never to lose.

The toaster rebels, makes bread fly high,
While fish in top hats eat pie in the sky.
A cactus recites poetry under the moon,
While a snail takes a taxi—yes, I'm immune!

Mondays are parties, emojis in suits,
With rulers as dancers in high-heeled boots.
And just when you think you've seen it all,
A giraffe in pajamas will surely enthrall.

So let's twirl in strange circles, in hats made of dreams,
And laugh till we tumble, or burst at the seams.
For the uncanny is charming, as fun as can be,
In the wacky unknown, come dance wild and free!

Two Steps Back, One Leap Forward

I tripped on a mat, fell flat on my face,
But laughed as I got up, I know this place.
With socks that don't match and hair full of hair,
I might stumble again, but I don't really care.

A coffee spill dance, oh what a delight,
The mug's gone afoul, but it sure feels right.
For every small blunder, I give a big cheer,
In this wacky old journey, I'm happy, my dear.

So when life throws your plans in a jigsaw mess,
Just grab a good laugh, and try not to stress.
With each funny fumble, I find my own way,
Two steps in the mud, still seizing the day.

And when I do leap, it might look quite odd,
But every small hop feels just like a prod.
So here's to the missteps, may they come more and more,

For in this wild waltz, I'm always a bore.

Footfalls on Thorny Trails

I wandered down paths where the prickers reside,
With each step I take, I'm roped in for the ride.
Oh, the things I have seen, what a colorful sight,
Like the squirrel that scolded me, full of spite.

With each thorn that I dodge, it feels like a game,
A twist and a turn, but they all feel the same.
I'll leap over puddles and swing round a tree,
For every scraped knee, oh, how wild I be!

Each footfall, a story of laughter and pain,
Of riding on clouds then drenched in the rain.
But with every new stumble, I smile and I grin,
A joke in the moment, like a spin on a pin.

In this garden of chaos, I find my own tune,
With giggles and chuckles and a sometimes monsoon.
So dance through the thorns, let the giggles commence,
For falling is winning, it just makes more sense.

A Garden of Grit and Grace

In a garden so wild, where the weeds like to play,
I pick up my trowel, hip-hip-hooray!
With dirt on my hands and mud on my shoes,
I'll plant all my dreams, I've got nothing to lose.

The roses come out with a snicker and tease,
While the daisies just giggle in the soft summer breeze.
Yet I prune and I tend, each tough little sprout,
Growing petals of laughter where there once was a drought.

The sun shines above, making shadows we chase,
With butterflies dancing in a comical race.
And when things get challenging, oh how I'll grin,
For that's where the beauty of grit can begin.

So here's to the blossoms that weather the storm,
With hearts full of joy, in every sweet form.
In this garden of grit, oh, I shall embrace,
The laughter, the mischief, the glorious grace.

The Thorns Beneath the Roses

Amidst lovely blossoms, thorns are nearby,
Oh, the tales they could tell with a laugh and a sigh.
For every sweet fragrance hides prickles that sting,
A reminder that life's often wrapped in a fling.

The roses might flaunt their beautiful blooms,
While the thorns roll their eyes, in dark, shady rooms.
In laughter we find that it's all intertwined,
One minute I'm up, the next in a bind.

Yet, prickly encounters are part of the game,
With bruises and chuckles, I'll never feel shame.
For every sharp bump just adds to the fun,
In this rollicking race, I'm still number one!

So let's lift up our glasses to moments absurd,
With a wink and a nod, to the wits that we've spurred.
For the thorns will be there, but so will the cheer,
In the dance of the bloom, let's laugh without fear.

The Grief of Unturned Stones

Oh, the rocks that dodge the sun,
They wish they'd had more fun.
Stuck in shadows, lost in gloom,
  Waiting for a chance to bloom.

Once a pebble with great dreams,
Now a footnote in stone memes.
If only they could break the trend,
  Maybe then they'd win a friend.

Boulders grumble, cracks do sigh,
Each chipped edge a whispered lie.
They gather dust, yet gleam with pride,
  Hoping for a joyful ride.

From nestled beds of dirt and grass,
They ponder why the moments pass.
With every tumble, there's a groove,
In their sorrow, they find their move.

Between the Cracks of Stone Hearts

In a world where hearts are stone,
Laughter's an adventure known.
Chipping away at icy shells,
Each jest a drop, it tells and swells.

They tried to hug, but missed instead,
A thump, a bump, and off they fled.
Yet in the cracks, the humor grows,
Just like a weed, nobody knows.

With each retort that flies so high,
These hardened hearts, they crack and sigh.
For laughter wears a softer face,
Among the stones, there's hidden grace.

So here we stand, a motley crew,
Seeking warmth as stones will do.
With every chuckle, sparks of light,
In cracks, new friendships take to flight.

The Turn of the Unfortunate Wheel

Round and round the wheel spins fate,
Sometimes it laughs, sometimes it's late.
One moment joy, the next a wipe,
It's just a game of misfortunate hype.

Tossed in a swirl of jumbled jest,
The wheel can leave you quite distressed.
But twist it once, and you might see,
The funny side of calamity.

Spinning tales of woe and glee,
Each turn reveals absurdity.
Though fortune's fickle, we can't despair,
With humor's balm, we'll rise from there.

So gather round for one more spin,
A touch of chaos wrapped in a grin.
Let's toast to mischief, let's celebrate,
For in this madness, it's never too late.

Beneath the Weight of Shrouded Layers

Beneath the layers, quirks reside,
Each moment cloaked, a merry ride.
A slip, a fall, a comic bluff,
Life's fabric woven from the tough.

In layers thick, the laughter hides,
As stumbles sprout and joy abides.
Each fumble wrapped in fabrics dense,
Turns mishaps into pure suspense.

So pull aside the veils so grey,
Let chuckles chase the gloom away.
In every fold, absurdity waits,
With every layer, laughter creates.

So when you're burdened by heavy shrouds,
Remember the jesters in the crowds.
For underneath the weight we bear,
There's humor twinkling everywhere.

The Beauty of Unplanned Moments

A cat on the roof, what a sight!
Chasing the birds in pure delight.
But down comes the pot, oh what a mess,
Now there's more to clean than we could guess.

Forgotten our keys, in the fridge they lie,
Wonder how they got there, oh my, oh my!
Yet laughing we are, with smiles so wide,
In the chaos around, our hearts open wide.

A trip to the store, planned out by the book,
Ended with snacks and one silly cook.
Who would have thought, such thrill could be found,
In the marvel of madness that's all around?

The dance of mishaps, our feet fumble and trip,
Yet we share out loud, and both laugh and skip.
For in every blunder, there's joy to be found,
In the beauty of chaos, love does abound.

Threads of Resilience Woven with Regret

Stitches like lightning, my sweater too tight,
Completed what started as a little fright.
A pattern of chaos, yet still worn with pride,
Though it's a snug fit, I'll be warm through the ride.

Tripping on air, what a glorious fall!
With dignity lost, I just giggle and crawl.
Regret's in a corner, laughing with glee,
As I shake off the earth, and set myself free.

I baked a fine cake, or so I had thought,
Instead got a muffin, and one little knot.
Yet friends gather 'round, with forks at the ready,
Our shared little laughter helps keep us steady.

Life's odd little quirks, poke fun at our fate,
Yet through every slip, we learn to create.
In the tapestry woven from threads of our blunders,
Resilience shines bright, past all of life's thunders.

The Tempest's Whisper

With winds in a rage, my hat took a flight,
Followed it sharply, what a silly sight!
Through puddles I splashed, like a cheerful fool,
The storm had its fun, while I played the tool.

A phone call, a mishap, they've lost my bag,
And here I am laughing, feeling quite swags!
Regrets float away, like the clouds in a race,
In this tempest's whisper, I find my true place.

Dinner was planned, but oh, what a mess,
Burned the main course, can you even guess?
Yet pizza arrives, it's a twist in the tale,
As we cheer for the pie, cherishing our gale.

Oh, storms may come, but I'll dance in the rain,
With puddles to splash, shedding all the pain.
In laughter's sweet rhythm, I join with the wind,
For even in chaos, my joy won't rescind.

Shadows on the Path

We wander through life with a curious gait,
Finding odd shadows, and giggling at fate.
An umbrella misplaced, now it's raining cats,
While dodging the puddles, and jumping like rats.

Stumbling on curbs, and laughing at stones,
Making up stories of lost little bones.
For every misstep, a tale to be spun,
In the dance of our days, mischief's begun.

A simple wrong turn leads to the best sights,
Like finding a café that serves moonlit bites.
So here's to the shadows, the bumps on the way,
Where smiles are found, come what may.

In the theater of life, we play our own parts,
Each stumble and giggle, forging our arts.
With shadows in tow, we'll laugh through it all,
For joy lives in moments, through every downfall.

www.ingramcontent.com/pod-product-compliance
Lightning Source LLC
Chambersburg PA
CBHW051631160426
43209CB00004B/603